Grace Kelly

A LIFE IN PICTURES

Grace Kelly

A LIFE IN PICTURES

Jenny Curtis

MetroBooks

MetroBooks

An Imprint of Friedman/Fairfax Publishers

© 1998 by Michael Friedman Publishing Group, Inc.

Library of Congress Cataloging-in-Publication data available upon request.

ISBN 1-56799-646-9

Editor: Francine Hornberger
Art Director: Kevin Ullrich
Layout Designer: Meredith Miller
Photography Editor: Sarah Storey
Production Manager: Ingrid Neimanis-McNamara

Color separations by Ocean Graphic International Company Ltd.
Printed in China by Leefung-Asco Printers Ltd.

10 9 8 7 6 5 4 3 2 1

For bulk purchases and special sales, please contact:
Friedman/Fairfax Publishers
Attention: Sales Department
15 West 26th Street
New York, NY 10010
212/685-6610   FAX 212/685-1307

Visit our website:
http://www.metrobooks.com

Dedication

For Chris

CONTENTS

Introduction

Above: Grace Kelly and Louis Jourdan share a dance in *The Swan* (1956). The elegant white formal gown that she wore in this scene was designed by MGM costume designer Helen Rose, who also designed Grace's wedding and bridesmaids' dresses.

Opposite: Grace gives a playful poolside smile in Hollywood, 1954. After finishing *Mogambo* (1953), for which she was nominated for an Academy Award, she read and rejected a number of scripts from MGM. She was always willing to wait for a part that she wanted to play and rarely caved in to studio pressure.

When Grace Kelly landed her first important role in the movies, she was twenty-one years old. She played Amy Kane, the naive Quaker bride of Gary Cooper, in the classic western *High Noon* (1952). In one scene, Cooper pulls her into an office, away from a crowd of well-wishers. He kicks the door shut, saying, "All those people. We oughta be married in private."

It is a sweet, romantic moment in the movie and one that bears incredible irony given Grace's marriage to Prince Rainier of Monaco a few years later. Grace's wedding on April 19, 1956, was dubbed "The Wedding of the Century," by members of the press, who covered it more closely than they had the Coronation of Elizabeth II of England in 1953.

The wedding of Hollywood's most popular female star and a real-life Prince Charming thrust Grace Kelly into a frenzy of international media attention that continued relentlessly until her untimely death in 1982. From the day Grace decided to leave Hollywood to become Princess of Monaco, paparazzi began throwing themselves at her, causing no end of distress to her and her family. Even after she made *High Noon*, Grace was seldom recognized and could still wander freely around New York, where she was surrounded by a pack of close friends and confidants. Nothing could have prepared her for the enormous change that was about to take place in her life.

While the press repeatedly described her marriage as "fairy tale," Grace went from highly successful career woman with a demanding, glamorous job to housewife overnight. Although she was hardly an ordinary hausfrau at her palace in Monaco, she was suddenly removed from her safety net of friends and family and thrust into a new world where she didn't speak the language or understand the intricacies of court protocol. Grace was used to a circle of friends who were privy to her wit and prankish sense of humor, but in Monaco, her only friend was her husband, who was consumed with the daily business of being the absolute ruler of his country. Despite her early difficulties as Serene Highness Princess

Opposite: A studio publicity shot for *High Noon* (1952) featuring a twenty-two-year-old Grace Kelly. Grace was far from content to rest on the film's success. Her performance did not stand out with critics, and she decided she needed to improve her craft so she returned to New York to get more acting experience.

Left: Grace Kelly in 1954. Her career was on the rise. After *Mogambo*, she appeared on the cover of *Life* magazine. The headline, "1954: The Year of Grace Kelly," uncannily predicted her meteoric rise from second-string parts to starring roles in some of the best pictures of the decade.

of Monaco, however, Grace raised a family and eventually adapted to her new duties, which included making light dinner conversation with people like President Kennedy and Charles de Gaulle.

On the surface, the story of how Grace Kelly became a movie star and then a princess seems to be one of extraordinary good fortune. However, Grace was a shrewd strategist, taking only the opportunities she felt would ultimately serve her best and making personal sacrifices to meet what she felt was her destiny. There was also a lot of hard work along the way, although Grace always made it look easy.

Grace acquired her gift for strategy and her determination from her parents. Her father was Irish Catholic, a former rowing champion who built the family business, Kelly Bricks, into a national concern. Her mother was a German Catholic nurse who was an efficient, vital part of her husband's growing political and social aspirations. Grace was born on November 12, 1929, into a family of extroverts and athletes. She is remembered by her family as being a shy, awkward child, prone to colds and apt to spend a lot of time

on her own with her dolls. Her greatest ally in the Kelly clan was her Uncle George, a famous playwright, from whom Grace garnered her refined taste and elegant, cool manner. Even as a child, Grace always dreamed of a cosmopolitan lifestyle for herself as an actress, filled with travel and exciting, glamorous people. But she never dreamed she would become a princess.

The Kellys were upper middle class, but were unable to join mainline Philadelphia Society because they were Catholic. Contrary to popular belief, Grace was not a debutante. By becoming a princess, of course, she went beyond her parents' wildest social aspirations. But that was like Grace—perhaps her shyness caused people to underestimate her. When she attended the American Academy of Dramatic Arts in New York following high school, her parents assumed it would be only a matter of weeks before she returned to Philadelphia to get married and start a family like her older sister Peggy. No one dreamed that "Gracie," as her family called her, would become an international legend.

Part One

Grace Kelly

Above: Grace Kelly, age three, in snow pants outside the Kelly home in Germantown, Pennsylvania. Even at this young age, it is evident how easily and freely Grace laughed. Her cool, sophisticated screen persona was one that often just barely managed to suppress her giggles.

Opposite: Portrait of Grace, twelve years old. As a young girl, Grace loved the movies and she often went to revivals of *Gone with the Wind* (1939). Her favorite actors were her future costars—Clark Gable, William Holden, and Ray Milland. In Hollywood in her twenties, Grace was romantically linked to all three of these men.

ight: Grace and her younger sister Lizanne in 1933. Grace was the second youngest in a family of four children. She and Lizanne are most often pictured together. They shared a room for years—as well as the typical battles that went with it. Lizanne once locked Grace in a closet for several hours and was amazed that Grace didn't complain or tattle on her. Grace had barely noticed. She was busy in her make-believe world, playing with her dolls.

eft: Grace and Lizanne all dressed up, circa 1936. Grace modeled professionally in New York before acting in movies, but her true love was the theater. Her childhood acting fantasies and amateur theatrics for the benefit of neighborhood audiences had a family tradition behind them. Two of her father's brothers were in show business. Her Uncle Walter was a famous vaudevillian, while her Uncle George was a playwright of note in the early half of the twentieth century.

pposite: The Kelly family enjoys their traditional summer retreat in Ocean City, New Jersey. From left to right, Grace's parents Jack and Margaret, Peggy, Jack, Jr. or "Kell," Grace, and Lizanne. Peggy, the oldest, was charismatic, and was considered to be the beauty of the family. Kell became an Olympic rower like his father. Born between Peggy and the baby, Lizanne, Grace suffered a bit from middle-child syndrome. Neighbors remember Peggy dragging Grace around by her hair. But Grace got no such satisfaction from Lizanne, who was willful one minute and charming their parents with her cuteness the next.

Grace Kelly, age seventeen, dances with her father. Their relationship was far from ideal. Her sister Lizanne recalls Grace competing with Peggy and Kell for their father's attention from the start. Nothing Grace could do seemed to inspire his confidence in her. Grace's paramour and instructor at the American Academy of Dramatic Arts, Don Richardson, said that Grace married Rainier to "make a bigger splash than an oar," in reference to John Kelly's devotion to his son's rowing career. Oleg Cassini said that Grace's father viewed her like "a racehorse. Something to be invested." These two suitors and potential husbands had reason to dislike Grace's father, as he disapproved of both of them. At different times, Grace brought Richardson and Cassini home to meet the family, partly to test the waters for marriage, but met with major resistance from her father. Both were divorced and Jewish, which made them unsuitable marriage material in the eyes of the Catholic Kellys.

Left: Grace Kelly, bathing beauty, age seventeen, perched modestly poolside. Grace left Pennsylvania in 1947 to study acting at the New York Academy of Dramatic Arts. She had some experience, having been in a Philadelphia production of her uncle's play, *The Torchbearers*. Her entrance notes to the Academy gave her high marks in stage presence and concentration, but she scored low on her voice, which was considered too weak and nasal for the stage.

Below: Grace and Lizanne wish Kell luck as he vies for the family dream of putting the Kelly name on the diamond sculls at Henley, England, in 1947. The famed rowing trophy had been denied his father, who was not allowed to compete because of an old rule that required competitors to be of the "gentleman" class. By the time Kell came of age, there were no such restrictions. Kell won that day, and like his father, he also went on to row in the Olympics. Lizanne would marry and start a family with an accountant, Donald Levine, soon after this picture was taken.

Above and opposite: Grace played Bertha in a Broadway production of August Strindberg's *The Father* (1950), starring Raymond Massey, who also directed. The play closed after two months, although Grace received favorable notices for her performances. After completing her training at the American Academy of Dramatic Arts in New York, Grace's career got off to a quick start. She moved from amateur to the top of professional theater in an astoundingly short time. Just days after graduation, she landed her first job as a professional actress with a place in the summer repertory company of the Bucks County (Pennsylvania) Playhouse. When she completed summer stock, Grace returned to New York to audition for *The Father*.

Opposite: Grace in her modeling days in New York. She used modeling to supplement her income and gain financial independence from her parents. Around this time, Grace also made a splash socially in New York. She was once escort to the Shah of Iran for a week. He presented her with jewels, which she kept (despite her parents' wishes) until she married Prince Rainier.

Above: Grace Kelly and costar in her film debut in *Fourteen Hours* (1951). Grace won a small role in this suicide drama that told the story of Robert Cosick (Richard Basehart), a young man who brings work in an office building to a halt for a whole day as he contemplates jumping from a window ledge. Grace played Mrs. Fuller, a woman who wants a divorce and who has a change of heart about her marriage after witnessing Cosick's struggle. Paul Douglas played Charlie Dunnigan, the policeman who tries to talk Cosick down from the ledge.

Left: Grace in a publicity photo for *Fourteen Hours*. Although praised by critics, the film did not fare well at the box office. Grace's part was so small it went virtually unnoticed. Still the studio was pleased with her work. After successfully completing the movie for 20th Century Fox, she was offered a stock contract, which she declined in order to return to New York and her true love, the theater.

Above: Aging sheriff Will Kane (Gary Cooper) marries the young and innocent Amy (Grace) in Stanley Kramer's classic western *High Noon* (1952). The film marked a great comeback for Cooper and was Grace's big break. Director Fred Zinneman attempted to make the details as realistic as possible by hiring Cooper, who was ill and showing his age, to play the sheriff. On the day of his retirement, the sheriff is forced to defend a town against a vicious gang arriving on the noon train. Grace was cast because her inexperience and obvious reserve were perfect for the part of the Quaker bride who must choose between her nonviolent beliefs and her feelings for her husband. Cooper brought a quiet severity and appealing vulnerability to his part, while Grace exhibited the radiant purity and reserve that became part of her film persona.

Right: Amy Kane and the sheriff's old girlfriend, Helen Ramirez (Kay Juarado), decide to leave town before the trouble starts. Helen has told Amy that the townspeople have abandoned the sheriff and that it is likely he will be killed. Amy is unable to convince Kane to shirk his duty and leave town with her, so she decides to save herself.

Left: After hearing gunshots, Amy gets off the train and runs to investigate. In this suspenseful shot, the audience is left guessing as to whether the figure in the dirt is the sheriff.

Right: Grace Kelly in a publicity photo promoting *High Noon*. One might think filming the movie was like a vacation on a dude ranch. Although Grace and her chaperon, her sister Lizanne, enjoyed the amenities of the Hollywood movie set, as well as jaunts in Cooper's Jaguar, Grace took her job very seriously and worked hard. When asked later whether he knew Grace would be a great actress, Gary Cooper said, "She had her eyes and ears open. She was trying to learn. You could see that. You can tell if a person really wants to be an actress. She was one of those people."

eft: Ava Gardner, Grace Kelly, and Clark Gable in *Mogambo* (1953). A remake of Gable's Depression-era romantic adventure, *Red Dust* (1932), *Mogambo* is a tangled love story involving anthropologist David Nordley (Donald Sinden); his wife, Linda (Grace); Victor Marswell (Gable), the big game hunter they hire as a guide in the African jungle; and Honey Bear, a shipwrecked showgirl (Gardner). Grace and Clark Gable were inseparable during the filming. The news of a romance between the two did not leak to the press until the couple reached London to complete the film. Grace said of the affair, "What else is a girl to do living in a tent with Clark Gable for five months?"

elow: Grace Kelly as the damsel in perpetual distress, Linda Nordley, in *Mogambo*. The role didn't offer much for Grace, but she played it with such a palpable sense of longing that it earned her a Best Supporting Actress nomination.

Opposite: Grace Kelly and Clark Gable in London. Publicly, the couple tried to quash the rumors of an affair with the standard reply: "We're just good friends." Gable added that he'd "never been so flattered," that is, by the suggestion that he and Grace were involved. He was fifty-two; Grace was only twenty-five at the time.

Above: Robert Cumming as Mark Halliday, Grace Kelly as Margot Wendice, and Ray Milland as Tony Wendice in *Dial M for Murder* (1954). Margot is a wealthy woman who is having an affair with Mark. Tony wants to have Margot killed because he fears that she will divorce him and he'll lose his meal ticket.

Left: Patrick Allen as the killer, Pearson, poises to attack Margot in *Dial M for Murder*. Hitchcock had wanted to shoot the scene with Grace wearing an elaborate velvet robe, but Grace felt it was unrealistic for her character to put one on just to answer the phone in her own apartment. The twenty-five-year-old newcomer stood up to the notoriously stubborn director and got her way. She played the scene in her nightgown, which made her character seem even more vulnerable. From that point on, Grace was given control over her wardrobe, hair, and makeup on all Hitchcock films.

Right: Margot fends off Pearson. Although she is at a disadvantage, Margot manages to kill her attacker with a pair of scissors. This scene marked the moment when Grace Kelly let her own wiry strength and unyielding determination first surface on screen. The patrician façade that she'd worn in previous films cracked as Hitchcock brought out a new side of her persona. Grace believed her performance in *High Noon* was wooden, but the physical struggle in *Dial M for Murder* forced her to move beyond dialogue and stage direction. Here, at last, was a real actress who let her emotions show on her face and in her tortured body language.

Right: Grace Kelly and Ray Milland pose for a publicity photo for *Dial M for Murder*. Grace was romantically linked with Ray Milland, who was married at the time. Whether there was anything serious behind the whirlwind of gossip surrounding the two stars, the label "home wrecker" was not something Grace wanted attached to her reputation. She broke off their friendship after the shooting was complete and passed off the whole "affair" as a simple misunderstanding.

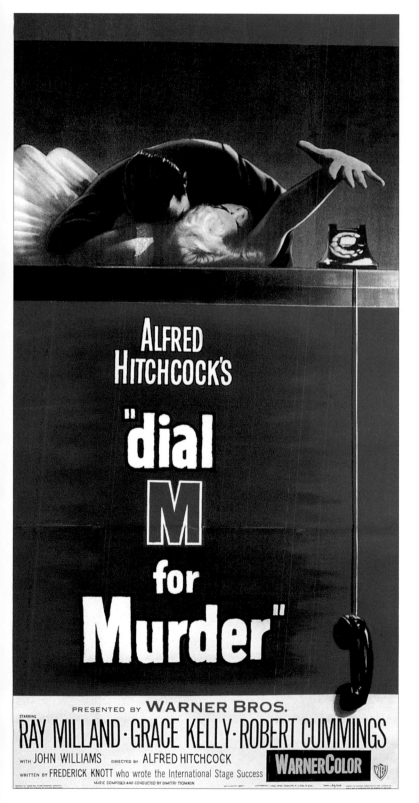

Left: Movie poster for Hitchcock's thriller, *Dial M for Murder* (1954). Ingrid Bergman had recently left Hollywood, leaving Hitchcock without a leading lady to play the cool blonde characters he was so fond of putting in danger on the screen. Grace Kelly not only matched Bergman's screen presence, but under Hitch's careful direction, she became the prototypical Hitchcock heroine.

Above: Grace dines with Spencer Tracy at an MGM dinner in 1954. She highly respected the older generation of actors and learned a lot about her craft from them. Although she was lucky enough to work with some of her heroes, she never acted with Tracy.

Right: Grace tries to keep a straight face with actor Danny Kaye during one of Hitch's famous tea breaks on the set of *Rear Window* (1954).

ight: Grace Kelly and Jimmy Stewart in a publicity photo for *Rear Window*. Although it appears that Stewart is showing Grace how to work the camera, Grace was the photographer in real life. She loved taking pictures and often practiced her hobby while on location. Grace always sought artistic ways to relax. As a child, she chose dancing as a creative outlet, and after retiring from acting, she made pressed flower collages that were good enough to be displayed in a museum in Paris.

elow: Grace presents Jimmy Stewart with a cast from "the cast" of *Rear Window*. Although happily married to his wife Gloria, he still appreciated Grace's charm. He answered critics who called her "the Ice Queen" with typical Stewart folksy wit: "Why, Grace is anything but cold—she has those big warm eyes. And well, if you ever have played a love scene with her, you'd know she's not cold."

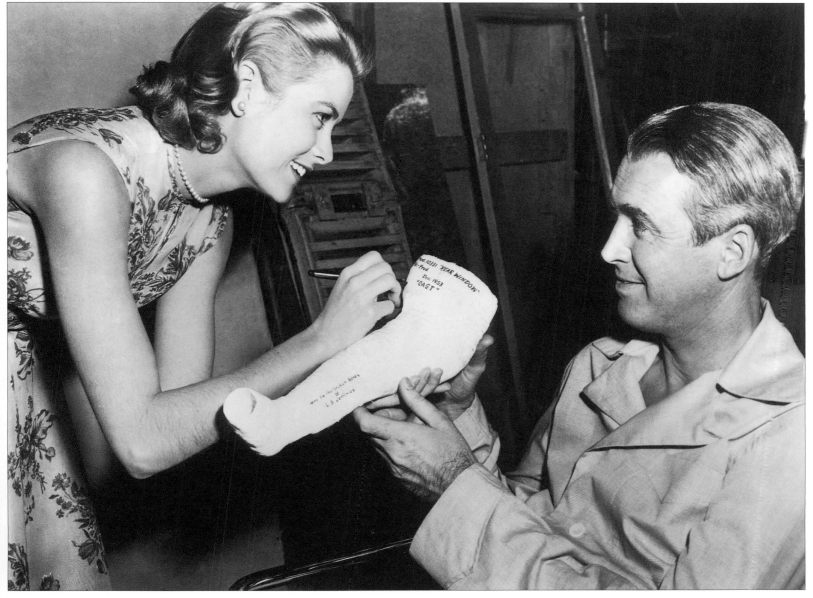

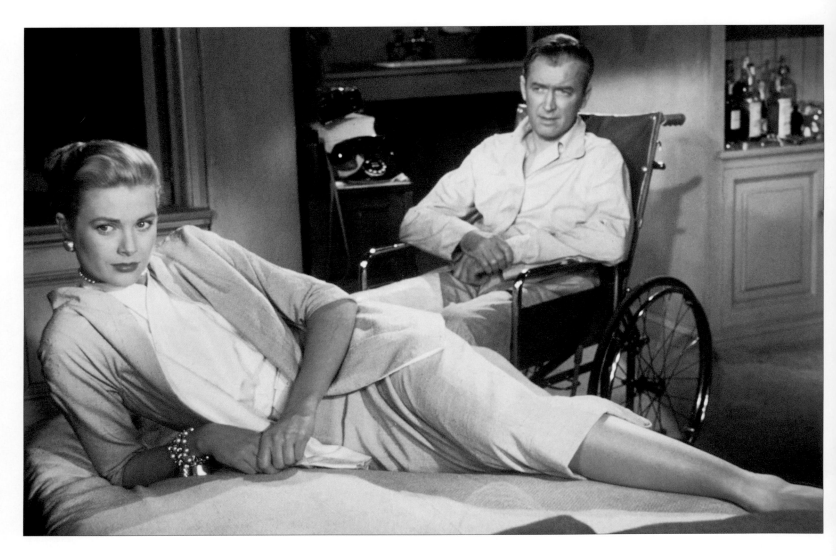

Opposite, top: Jimmy Stewart and Grace Kelly stare out the infamous "rear window" in Hitchcock's classic thriller. Grace played Lisa Fremont, a Park Avenue fashion model, whose photographer boyfriend, L.B. Jeffries (Jimmy Stewart), witnesses a murder from his Greenwich Village apartment.

Opposite, bottom: As the movie rolls on, it is revealed that each window in Jeffries' apartment complex contains a tidy subplot, and it is not until Lisa and Jeff begin to unravel the mystery that the stories become intertwined. Lisa is at first appalled by her boyfriend's voyeuristic behavior, but eventually she becomes intrigued by the mystery and helps him catch the killer by going places he can't because of his broken leg.

Above: Grace Kelly and Jimmy Stewart attend the *Rear Window* premiere at the Hollywood Paramount Theater on August 11, 1954.

Opposite: Grace, circa 1954. Grace's glamour and urbane presence had started to earn her success and respect, but she was always cast in the same type of role. Stereotyping was acceptable, even desirable, in the Hollywood of the 1930s and 1940s, but Grace was a star during the 1950s when studios were keeping fewer employees and those who remained were expected to be versatile. Grace's childhood idol and recent costar, Clark Gable, had been laid off. If MGM could fire "The King," Grace knew she needed to prove that she could play more than one type to keep working.

Above: Grace Kelly as Georgie Elgin in *The Country Girl* (1954). To move from her glamorous patrician persona to an earthy, frumpy character was a leap for Grace. She pulled it off, and the role established her as a serious, dramatic actress in Hollywood. It also won her the Oscar for Best Actress that year.

Left: William Holden as Broadway producer Bernie Dodd, Grace Kelly as Georgie Elgin, and Bing Crosby as Georgie's husband Frank. At first it seems as if Georgie is an overwrought, domineering, and even sinister woman. But eventually it is revealed that her husband is a manipulative, pathetic alcoholic, making Georgie seem noble and resilient.

Right: Grace photographs costar Bing Crosby with her favorite Roleflex camera. Grace and the recently widowed Crosby dated for a while during the filming of *The Country Girl*. Grace's chaperon on those dates, her sister, Lizanne, said that Bing was "daffy about Grace," but the feeling wasn't mutual.

Grace Kelly with her brother and father at *The Country Girl* premiere. Grace's career as a film star surprised her father, who had known success in business, athletics, and politics. "Grace is the last of my children who I thought would support me in my old age," he said.

Opposite: Grace Kelly accepts the Best Actress Oscar for *The Country Girl*. By the time the Academy Awards ceremony rolled around, Grace was on suspension from MGM for failing to make a second picture for the studio. She had been on perpetual loan-out for two years, while continuing to regularly reject MGM scripts. After she won this award, however, the studio dropped her suspension.

Left: Grace Kelly and William Holden on the set of *The Bridges at Toko-Ri* (1954), the story of a lawyer, Harry Brubaker (Holden), who is called to service flying planes for the Navy in Japan during the Korean War.

Right: Grace Kelly takes direction from Mark Robson in *The Bridges at Toko-Ri* (1954). Although it was a Korean war movie that was filmed for the most part on location in the Far East, Grace's character, Nancy Brubaker, still had a large role. Her scenes were filmed in Hollywood.

Left: William Holden and Grace Kelly as Harry and Nancy Brubaker in *The Bridges at Toko-Ri*. This scene was a fairly intimate one for its day, although Holden is observing the Hayes Code (the production code that governed the content and spirit of Hollywood movies from the 1930s until the late 1950s), which stated in effect that if a couple is in the same bed together, one of them must keep at least one foot on the floor.

Right: Stewart Granger combs Grace's hair between takes of *Green Fire* (1954).

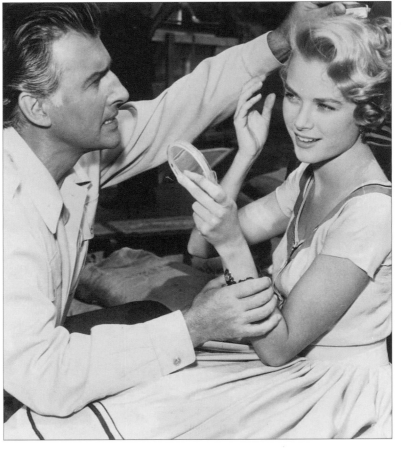

Opposite: Grace Kelly on a boat on the Magdelena River in Colombia during the filming of *Green Fire*. To compete with television, Hollywood sought to hang on to audiences by providing the glamour of travel in exotic locations. Filmed in Technicolor, *Green Fire* was the type of entertainment that the small screen could not yet provide. But the travelogue beauty shown on screen came at a price. The cast was nearly drowned shortly after this picture was taken, when the steering went out on the boat during a storm. Grace and the rest were rescued with dug-out canoes.

Above: Grace feeds coconut milk to a baby donkey in Sitionuevo, Colombia, in 1954. Although the picturesque location for *Green Fire* made for great photo opportunities, the shoot was long and grueling. Most of the cast and crew were ready to return to Hollywood long before it was complete.

Left: Grace on the set of *Green Fire* in 1954. Grace played the owner of a South American coffee plantation who falls in love with an emerald prospector (Stewart Granger). She didn't want to do this film, but was forced to because of her contractual obligation to MGM. If she refused, the studio would suspend her again.

Opposite: Rian Mitchell (Granger) and Catherine Knowland (Kelly) embrace after saving the plantation and finding the emerald at the end of *Green Fire*. Granger bragged in his autobiography that he groped Grace during this scene. If Grace noticed, she didn't complain. She was probably just relieved to finish the difficult, muddy scene.

Left: Grace even managed to look feminine and elegant in men's-style clothing and short hair, despite her slightly comical gentleman-of-the-manor pose with the hound in this picture.

Opposite: Grace Kelly in a sexy pose usually reserved for the bombshell types in 1955.

Left: A poster for *To Catch a Thief*. Director Alfred Hitchcock lured Cary Grant out of temporary retirement with the promise of a Riviera location and the opportunity to work with Grace Kelly.

Below: Grace Kelly and Cary Grant in a publicity photo for *To Catch a Thief* (1955). Grant plays John Robie, a former jewel thief who poses as an American businessman to catch a cat burglar and clear his own name. The daughter of a wealthy American oil tycoon, Frances Stevens (Kelly), is looking for a husband and an adventure. The success of the movie depended on the chemistry between Cary and Grace. Cary was concerned that he was too old for the part, but his lean, elegant, older face was the perfect contrast for Grace's smooth, youthful beauty.

Opposite: Grace snuggles up after a swim in her pool at home in Hollywood shortly before starting the filming of *To Catch a Thief* in 1955.

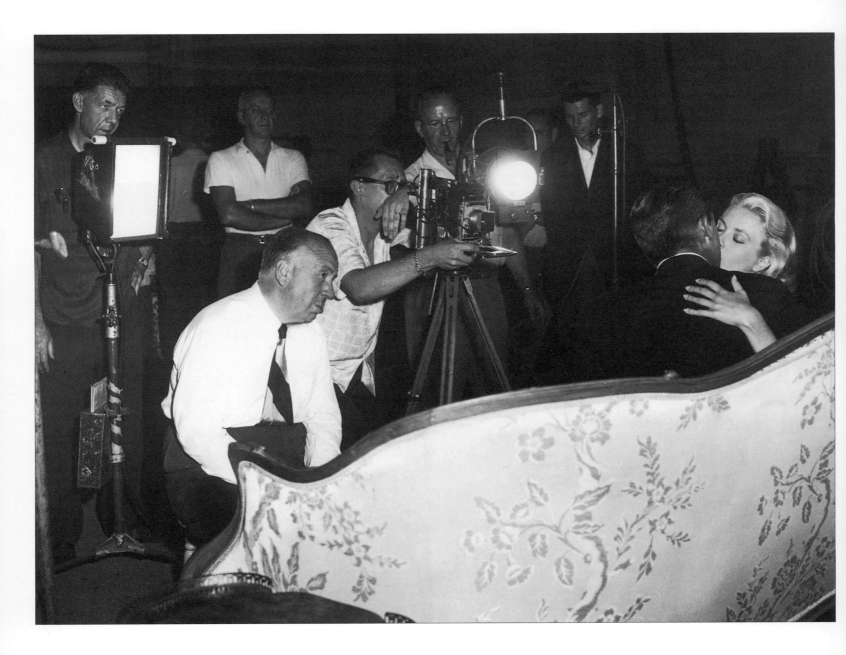

Above: Alfred Hitchcock directs Grace Kelly and Cary Grant in *To Catch a Thief*. Hitch appears a bit skeptical about the lipwork in the famous fireworks love scene. Critics noted that this film lacked the usual intensity and suspense of most Hitchcock movies, but it was greatly improved by the psychological tension of the love scenes.

Opposite: Grace looks perfectly at ease in her surroundings on the French Riviera during the filming of *To Catch a Thief*. The location provided her with her first glimpse of Monaco, which was to be her future home. During a break from shooting, Grace happened to drive by Prince Rainier's house and garden. Although she did not get the opportunity to meet her future husband on this trip, she marveled at his view of the Mediterranean.

Left: Grace and a makeup artist put on finishing touches before the fireworks love scene in *To Catch a Thief*. When Grace and Cary were spotted dining together in secluded restaurants on the Riviera, rumors began to fly about an on-the-set romance between the two stars. But Grant's wife, Betsey Drake, and Grace's boyfriend, Oleg Cassini, showed up on the set and stopped the wagging tongues. Grace became great friends with Cary and Betsey and spent a weekend with them in Palm Beach after the filming was complete. The Grants gave Grace her beloved poodle, Oliver, and Cary was one of her Hollywood friends who faithfully visited her in Monaco.

Right: A more typical Grace as she would often appear on the set—with camera and glasses. Grace was nearsighted, a problem for an actress in the pre–contact lens era.

eft: Frances Stevens (Kelly) watches John Robie (Grant) climb out of a speedboat and casually swim ashore. Stevens has not yet met Robie and is startled by his dark good looks and curious habit of jumping out of boats. It is her first clue that he is not what he claims to be when he is introduced to her as an American lumberman from Portland, Oregon.

elow: Grace and Cary film a swimming sequence for *To Catch a Thief*. The larger water camera is in the background. With effects added, this shallow pool appears to be the beach at Cannes.

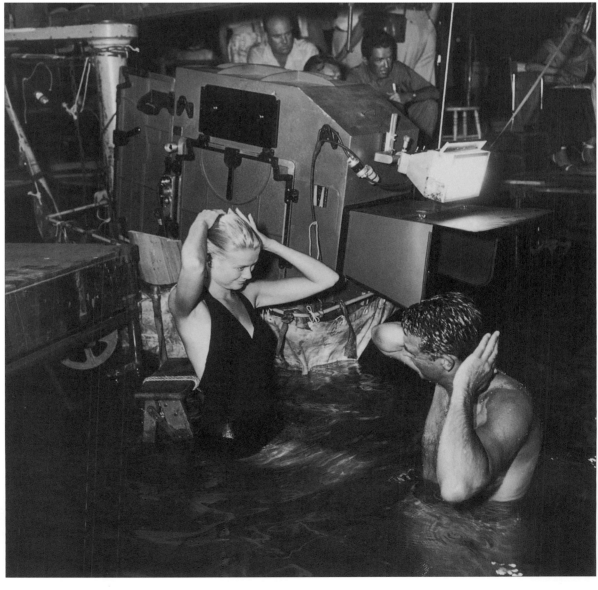

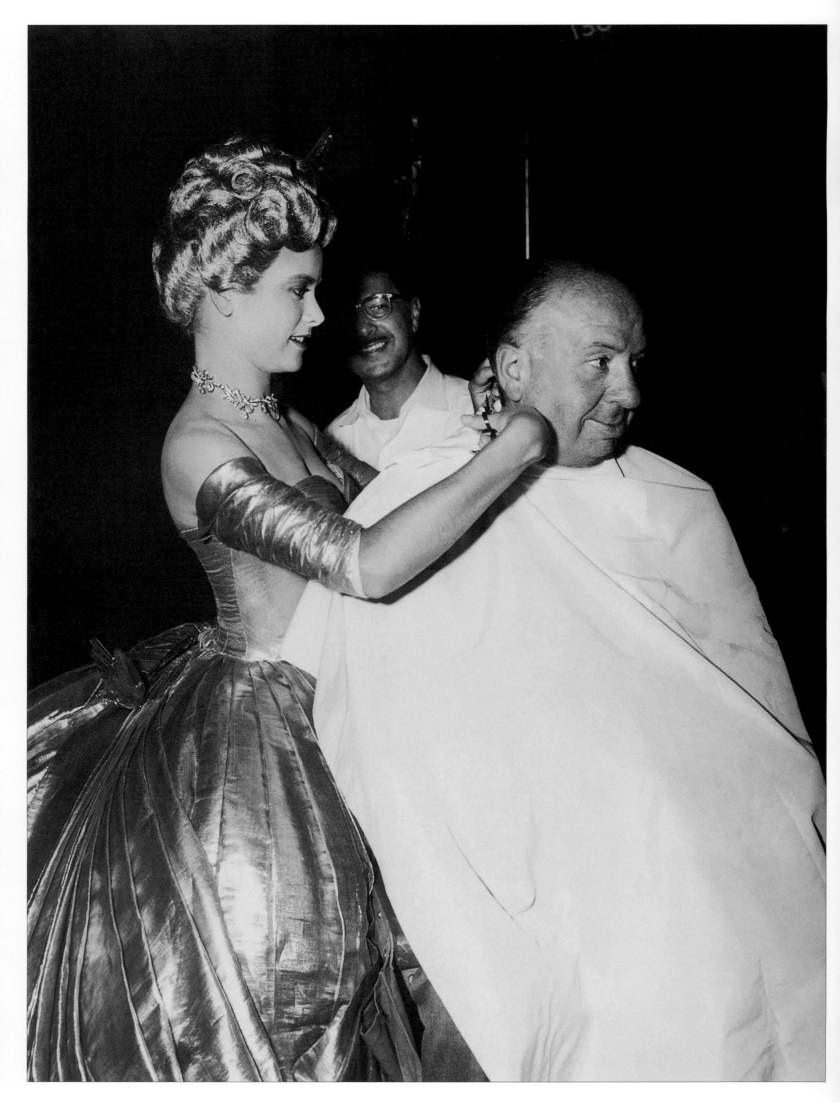

Opposite and left: Hitchcock had an unrequited crush on Grace that became an obsession. At left, he directs Grace while he fixes her gown. Grace was also very fond of Hitch, demonstrated in the photo on the opposite page, where she gives the legendary director a trim between takes. After Grace retired, Hitchcock attempted to turn some of his other leading ladies, such as Eva Marie Saint and Kim Novak, into re-creations of Grace Kelly.

Right: Grace proved that even in unflattering light, with no makeup, she was truly the golden girl.

Above: Grace hunts and pecks out a tune at her piano, circa 1955. Although Grace never had any formal musical training, she did enjoy playing for fun. Her natural ability stood her in good stead during the making of *High Society* (1956), when Grace sang successfully despite the studio's worries. Her duet with costar Bing Crosby, titled "True Love," sold a million copies.

Below: Grace Kelly and Oleg Cassini in 1955. The friendship between Grace and the famous designer blossomed into a passionate romance when he arrived on the Riviera during the filming of *To Catch a Thief*. The couple was secretly engaged, but Grace retreated from marriage after Oleg's first disastrous visit to meet her family in Philadelphia. The staunchly Catholic Kellys made no bones about his unsuitability as a potential husband. Grace and Oleg remained lifelong friends, but from interviews with him later on, it was obvious that he never quite got over her.

Above: A breathtaking portrait of Grace, circa 1955. The veil, reminiscent of brides and nuns, captures Grace's spirituality.

Below: Grace is photographed with a French artisan during a trip she took with French actor Jean-Pierre Aumont to Saint-Paul-de Vence, an artist colony near Cannes. The couple was so frequently photographed together during the 1955 Cannes Film Festival that when Grace returned to the United States, everyone, including her family, was convinced that Grace and Aumont were about to get engaged. Grace simply laughed it off. She was quietly impressed with Prince Rainier of Monaco, whom she'd met briefly at a publicity stunt during the festival.

Above: Grace arriving in Paris on her way to the 1955 Cannes Film Festival, where she was the official representative from Hollywood. Upon returning to New York, she sent Prince Rainier a polite "thank you" note, explaining how she'd enjoyed meeting him and touring his principality. Rainier used the note to open a correspondence with the film star, who was unmarried, beautiful, and Catholic—quite a catch for a prince desperately in search of a wife. Due to a clause in Monegasque law, the principality would revert back to French control if the prince could not produce an heir. In his autobiography, Rainier said that he was very impressed with Grace at their first short meeting and that she was different from what he'd expected. For her part, Grace said she "just knew" that there was something about Rainier that would be important to her in the future.

Opposite: Grace Kelly and Louis Jourdan on the set of *The Swan* in North Carolina, 1956. *The Swan* is the story of Princess Alexandra (Grace Kelly), who has trained her whole life to marry Crown Prince Albert (Alec Guiness), but falls in love with her fencing tutor, Nicholas Agi (Louis Jourdan). In the end, Alexandra forgoes the debonair but flighty younger man for the witty, older prince. Grace became engaged to Prince Rainier, who was five years older than she, over Christmas that year—just two weeks after *The Swan* was completed.

Above: Louis Jourdan as Nicholas Agi and Grace Kelly as Princess Alexandra in *The Swan*. While Jourdan was courting Grace on screen, Prince Rainier was courting her in real life. Their correspondence increased and so did the trans-Atlantic telephone calls. But it was their second meeting, in the relaxed atmosphere of the home of Kelly family friends, that set Grace and Rainier on the path toward marriage. They spent Christmas vacation together and by the New Year, they were engaged. Grace kept her relationship with Rainier a secret until after their engagement was announced, which led many in America to believe that the union was prearranged. Grace's Hollywood friends were shocked that she had made such a big decision without consulting anyone outside her family. Still, Grace had been contemplating marriage for a long time, and her family's rejection of Cassini as a potential husband had been a difficult blow. In Rainier, she finally had a suitor to which her family could have no objections.

Above: Grace Kelly and Alec Guinness examine the script for *The Swan*. The two became lifelong friends due to an on-location prank involving an ugly souvenir tomahawk, which Guinness and Kelly would take turns hiding in each other's quarters. Grace went so far as to smuggle it into Guinness's hotel room in Hollywood when he accepted the Oscar for *The Bridge on the River Kwai* (1957). The game continued until just before Grace's death.

Left: Louis Jourdan (left) and Grace Kelly take fencing lessons from Jean Heremans on the set of *The Swan* in 1956.

Right: Grace Kelly showed off her newly acquired fencing skills in this delightful scene in which swordplay becomes foreplay between the princess and her tutor.

Left: Grace Kelly and friend in the courtyard of the Vanderbilt estate in North Carolina where *The Swan* was filmed.

Opposite: Grace enjoys a good chortle during the filming of *The Swan* in North Carolina in 1956.

Right: Grace Kelly looking regal in *The Swan*. During the course of this scene, Princess Alexandra is given a final chance to redeem her earlier awkwardness with the prince, but she is so distracted by the attention of Nicholas that, to her mother's dismay, she leaves the dance unexpectedly with the young tutor.

GRACE KELLY 63

Above: Grace Kelly and Prince Rainier of Monaco announced their engagement at a New Year's party in 1956 at the Waldorf Astoria in New York. The news that Hollywood royalty was marrying real-life royalty set off a media frenzy. The Kelly home was swamped with reporters within days of the announcement. For the rest of her life, everything Grace did and said was considered newsworthy. The relative privacy she'd enjoyed as an actress in New York, and later as a star among dozens of other stars in Hollywood, was gone forever.

Opposite: Kelly family portrait taken shortly after the engagement in early 1956. Top row, left to right: Kell's wife, Mrs. John B. Kelly Jr.; Lizanne's husband, Donald Levine; Grace's brother, Kell; Peggy's husband, George Davis; and Grace's younger sister, Lizanne. Bottom row, left to right: Prince Rainier; Grace Kelly; Grace's parents, Margaret and John; and Grace's older sister, Peggy. Several of Grace's Hollywood friends who visited the Kelly home noticed a remarkable change in her personality when she was with her family. She again became the shy middle child. Her older sister Peggy leaps out of this picture, radiating the glamour and confidence Grace managed on the screen, while Grace retreats into herself even though she is the center of attention.

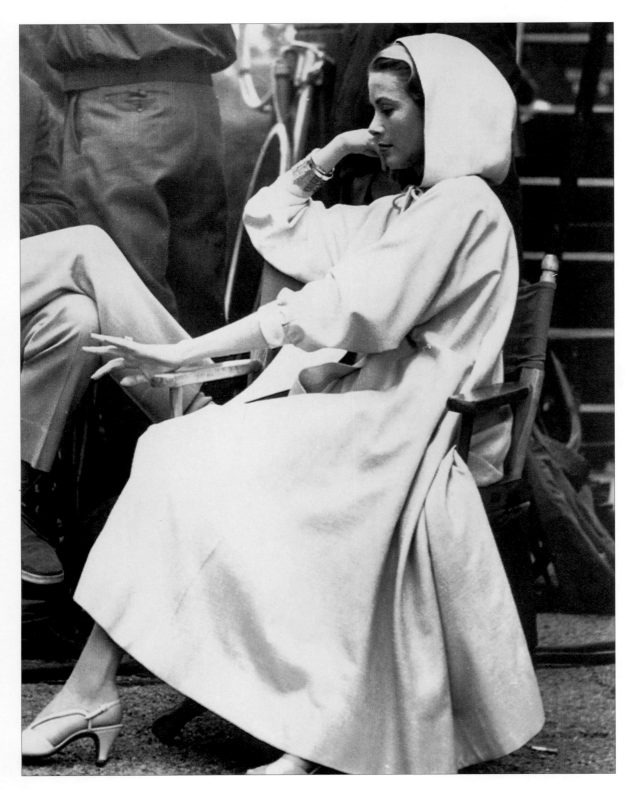

Above: Grace admires her engagement ring on the set of *High Society* (1956). Although her career as an actress was probably the best preparation she could have had for her upcoming role as princess, the intensity of her schedule didn't allow her much of a chance to savor her engagement.

Opposite: Frank Sinatra as Mike Connor, Bing Crosby as C.K. Dexter Haven, and Grace Kelly as Tracy Lord in *High Society*. Grace occasionally held mini–press conferences between takes to answer questions about her upcoming wedding to Prince Rainier of Monaco.

Left: Tracy Lord (Grace Kelly) gets tipsy on champagne with Mike Connor (Frank Sinatra) at a party the night before her wedding. *High Society* was a musical remake of the 1940 MGM classic *The Philadelphia Story*. Grace had big shoes to fill in taking on the role of Tracy Lord, which had been written for Katharine Hepburn, but she played the part of the Philadelphia heiress convincingly and handled the singing as well.

Opposite: Grace Kelly with Louis Armstrong who appeared as himself in *High Society*.

Right: *High Society* director Charles Waters amuses Grace on the set. Her future in Hollywood was up in the air in 1956. Grace was planning at least a temporary retirement, while her contract with MGM still required her to make two more films. Grace didn't plan to retire from Hollywood completely, but the demands of the role of princess meant that *High Society* would be the last feature film Grace Kelly ever made.

Below: Grace Kelly as Tracy Lord in *High Society*. Lord's ex-husband, Dexter (Crosby), accuses her of being a virginal goddess. The costume and the poolside pillars would seem to suggest the same.

Above: Mike and Tracy return from their "rather late swim" in *High Society*. Although the remake lacked the sparkle of the original film, at least Sinatra was better equipped to handle the crooning in this scene than Jimmy Stewart, whose drunken warbling of "Somewhere Over the Rainbow" in *The Philadelphia Story* had been played for comedy.

Portrait of Grace Kelly, circa 1956. Grace's cool beauty and screen goddess persona invited photographers to put her in a Hellenic setting.

Part Two

Princess Grace

Opposite: In April 1956, Grace Kelly was set to become Princess Grace of Monaco. Grace lent her glamour and visibility to a country that depended almost solely on tourism for its economic survival. Monaco had always been a favorite destination with the world's wealthiest people who, by 1956, had come to gamble at the famous casino in Monte Carlo for almost a century. Tourism increased noticeably from the day that Grace's engagement was announced, and for the first time ever, "daytrippers" from France were arriving in droves to see for themselves the beautiful principality on the Mediterranean.

Above: The very stunning Princess Grace. With her hair attended by the most exclusive Paris salons and clothes by Dior, Grace was always one of the most elegant women in the world. Still, it was her disarming friendliness and warmth that most impressed the so-called "Great Families" of Europe. Princess Grace and her family began to be accepted into the company of other royalty. Grace knew that these people were important to Monaco, and she formed genuine friendships with some of them, such as Earl Mountbatten, the uncle of the Prince of Wales.

Above: On April 4, 1956, Grace Kelly waved good-bye to her life in America. She's pictured here, moving through throngs of well-wishers and press, to board the U.S.S. *Constitution*, the boat that would take her to her new life in Monaco.

Left: Grace plays shuffleboard with her nieces, Margaret and Mary Lee Davis, aboard the U.S.S. *Constitution*. The media descended on Monaco, and as thousands held their breath, waiting for the nuptials to begin, banal photos such as this one became headline news around the world.

Below: Grace Kelly en route to Monaco. Grace's love of comfortable clothes earned her scorn from the European aristocracy, whose world she was about to enter. The Principality of Monaco was considered a minor dynasty at the time, and none of the "Great Families" of Europe attended the wedding.

Below: Grace Kelly arrives by limousine at the Cathedral of St. Nicholas for her wedding on April 19, 1956. Prince Rainier arrived a few minutes later in another car.

Above: Prince Rainier and Grace take their vows. The couple was legally wed in a private civil ceremony the day before, a necessity under Monegasque law. The very public church ceremony took place before the entire population of Monaco (about four thousand people) and MGM's movie cameras, which filmed the wedding as a partial fulfillment of her contract. MGM released the half-hour documentary, *The Wedding in Monaco*, which featured scenes from the wedding and the preceding celebrations, to cash in on the loss of one of their biggest stars. In return, Grace got their professional makeup, wardrobe, and publicity assistance.

Opposite: The newlyweds leave the Cathedral. By all accounts, the wedding was an ordeal for most involved because of the sheer size and complexity of the affair. Grace and Rainier seem completely thrilled to share a semiprivate moment in the busy day.

Above: Prince Rainier and Princess Grace, pregnant with Caroline, visit her old summer home in Ocean City, New Jersey, in September 1956. Grace was determined to raise her children with some American values and Kelly family traditions. For years, the prince and princess held a Sunday barbecue at the palace, with Rainier as head burger chef. Grace wanted her children to have normal childhoods. Rainier, too, was adamant that his children not be shuffled off to boarding schools as he had been.

eft: Grace with Princess Caroline in 1957. The birth of their first child, nine months after their wedding, took some of the pressure off Rainier and Grace. The principality had its heir, and Grace had proved that she could handle the transition from actress to princess.

elow: The first official photo of Princess Grace and her son, Prince Albert, born in March 1958. Albert superseded Caroline as the heir to the principality.

pposite: Princess Caroline, Prince Rainier, Princess Grace, and infant Prince Albert make up a royal family photo taken on the occasion of Albert's christening. Named Albert Alexandre Louis Pierre, Grace always called him Albie.

A merica's idea of royalty met the real thing when Grace and Rainier held court with President and Mrs. Kennedy in 1961.

Left: Grace, Caroline, and Albert on vacation in the Swiss Alps in 1962. During a holiday in Switzerland, Grace's beloved poodle Oliver was killed by another dog while Grace watched, horrified.

Below: Princess Grace at bat for Monaco's American Week in 1967. The glamour of Grace's movie-star presence in Monaco never wore off. She continued to attract tourists and jet-setters to the hotels and casinos of Monaco.

Left: Princess Caroline, Prince Rainier, Prince Albert, Princess Grace, and infant Princess Stephanie, born May 1965. The youngest of Grace's children, Stephanie often acted up and un-like her older sister Caroline, was completely uninterested in being a princess.

Left: Princess Grace with the nine-year-old Prince Albert. This serene portrait was taken poolside on holiday in Jamaica, in 1967. Grace and Albie were always very close. She worried that he would have problems growing up because of his special position in life, but Albert proved to be well adjusted and successful in his preparations to take over as absolute ruler of Monaco. Through the years, Prince Albert has demonstrated no desire to give up his bachelorhood to supply an heir to the principality.

Below: Eva Renzi, Prince Albert, Princess Caroline, Princess Grace, George Kennedy, and director Delbert Mann on the set of the movie *Jolly Pink Jungle*. Grace took her family to visit her former Hollywood haunts in 1967, long after she had said farewell. She toyed with the idea of returning to the movies on several occasions, but the outcry in Monaco made it more trouble than it was worth.

ight: Princess Stephanie and an exasperated Princess Grace in 1968. As Stephanie grew into a teenager, she became increasingly willful. At seventeen, she fell in love with a race-car driver from the Monaco Grand Prix. Grace was worried because both of her daughters tended to be attracted to the same types of men as she had been—older, worldly "playboy" types who brought a lot of potential heartbreak to their relationships. In 1995, Princess Stephanie married Daniel Ducruet, her former bodyguard and the father of her two children, Louis and Pauline, but the couple divorced in late 1997.

eft: From left to right: Prince Rainier, Princess Caroline, Princess Stephanie, Princess Grace, and Prince Albert. Grace made Rainier give up most of his death-defying hobbies, such as scuba diving and race car driving. Still, he continued to indulge his inner child by keeping a private zoo that included chimpanzees, African lions, and exotic snakes.

Above: Princess Caroline (left), Princess Grace holding Princess Stephanie, and Prince Albert on vacation in England in 1969. Grace loved to escape the perfect weather in Monaco to the gloom and relative anonymity of London. She and Rainier often went shopping in the fashionable Knightsbridge district as though they were just any other couple.

Left: Princess Grace and Princess Caroline in 1970. Years later, Princess Caroline joined the young jet set in Paris. When she completed high school, she became engaged to playboy Philippe Junot. Grace and Rainier were not pleased with Junot, who was a decade older than Caroline. The couple were married, but Caroline was granted an annulment after two years of experiencing Junot's philandering. She eventually remarried Stefano Casiraghi and had three children, Andrea, Charlotte, and Pierre. Casiraghi died in a boating accident in 1993. Caroline became an important figure in the principality after her mother's death, taking on responsibilities that her younger brother was not yet ready to handle.

Right: Princess Grace, Princess Stephanie, and Prince Rainier at the annual Monaco Red Cross Christmas party. Every year, the children of Monaco were invited to the palace to meet Santa Claus and the royal family.

Left: Princess Grace and Prince Albert accompany Princess Stephanie to her first day of school in 1971. Security guards stroll closely behind to protect the family from the danger of kidnapping.

Right: Princess Grace addresses the La Leche League in Chicago about the virtues of breast-feeding, 1971. La Leche stood out among the myriad of charities and organizations with which Grace was involved because it became something of a personal crusade for her. Grace was also active in the Red Cross, and in the Foundation that bears her name, which provided money for the arts.

Below: Princess Grace was a guest of Lady Diana and Prince Charles just following their engagement in 1981. Grace understood Diana's nervous, shy exterior better than anyone because she herself had been thrust into the royal goldfish bowl upon her own engagement in 1956. Charles and Di's wedding was also a worldwide media event. Grace must have understood the incredible pressures Diana was under and been sympathetic.

Above: In Hollywood, in Monaco, throughout the world, Grace Kelly was an icon of style, glamor, and unsurpassed charm, elegance, and grace.

Conclusion

Left: A royal family portrait.

Opposite: Princess Grace performs a poetry reading in 1980 as part of a series she did to raise funds for the Princess Grace Foundation, which provides money for the arts. She read Shakespeare in England, American classics on ABC television, and sponsored a celebration of Joyce's *Ulysses* with novelist and Joycean Anthony Burgess. Grace was very concerned that Monaco should have a cultural life beyond the casinos. She also loved the chance to perform before an audience.

On September 14, 1982, Princesses Grace and Stephanie set out from their summer home in Monaco, down the steep and treacherous road that was featured in *To Catch a Thief*. Grace suffered a minor stroke behind the wheel and lost control of the car. Although in shock, Stephanie, who suffered only minor injuries, left the car to summon help. Princess Grace died that night of injuries received in the accident. A few days later, in the Cathedral of St. Nicholas, where she and Rainier had been married, the world said good-bye to Grace Kelly, Princess of Monaco. The royals who had not come to her wedding were there in force, as a sign of how much Grace had meant to the principality and the world beyond it.

Grace's untimely death at age fifty-two created an outpouring of grief around the world. The many fans of her Hollywood career, even after twenty-five years of retirement, were saddened that her great talent was lost just as she was planning to return to the screen. In Monaco, the principality that had been her home for the latter half of her life, the people grieved in an uncharacteristically open manner. It was a sign that they had accepted the former American movie star, of whom they were at first so skeptical, as their princess.

Far from being just a pretty face, Grace brought a sense of style and class to everything she did. She was well-respected and adored, both as an actress and a royal. She was the picture of motherhood, the champion of several causes, and an international presence. The white gloves she wore as a young actress in New York were symbolic of the proper image she put forth to the public. They had a kind of quirky classiness, even in the 1950s, but they could be easily slipped off and set aside, like her public façade, when the private Grace wanted to come out to tell a joke or enjoy her favorite treats, hamburgers and pink champagne.

Filmography

Bibliography

MOTION PICTURES

Fourteen Hours, 20th Century Fox (1951).

High Noon, Stanley Kramer Productions (1952).

Mogambo, MGM (1953).

Rear Window, Paramount (1954).

Green Fire, MGM (1954).

Dial M for Murder, Warner Bros. (1954).

The Country Girl, Paramount (1954).

The Bridges at Toko-Ri, Paramount (1954).

To Catch a Thief, Paramount, (1955).

The Wedding in Monaco, MGM (1956).

High Society, MGM (1956).

The Swan, MGM (1956).

Invitation to Monte Carlo, Documentary (1959).

Poppies Are also Flowers, Wiener Standthallen Film (1966) (a.k.a. *Danger Grows Wild*, *The Opium Connection*, *The Poppy Is Also a Flower*)

Rearranged, unfinished, unreleased (1982)

TELEVISION

Hollywood Screen Test (1948).

The Web (1950) in episode: "Mirror of Delusion."

Studio One (1948) in episode: "The Rockingham Tea Set."

Philco Television Playhouse (1948) in episode: "Ann Rutledge."

Big Town (1950) in episode: "The Pay-Off."

Suspense (1949) in episode: "Fifty Beautiful Girls."

Danger (1950) in episode: "Prelude to Death."

Lux Video Theatre (1950) in episode: "A Message for Janice"

Once Upon a Time Is Now, NBC 1977.

Bradford, Sarah. *Princess Grace*. London: Weidenfeld and Nicolson, 1984.

Edwards, Anne. *The Grimaldis of Monaco*. New York: Morrow, 1992.

Englund, Steven. *Grace of Monaco: An Interpretive Biography*. Garden City, N.Y.: Doubleday, 1984.

Gaither, Gant. *Princess of Monaco: The Story of Grace Kelly*. New York: H. Holt, 1957.

Spada, James. *Grace: The Secret Lives of a Princess*. New York, Doubleday, 1987.

Index